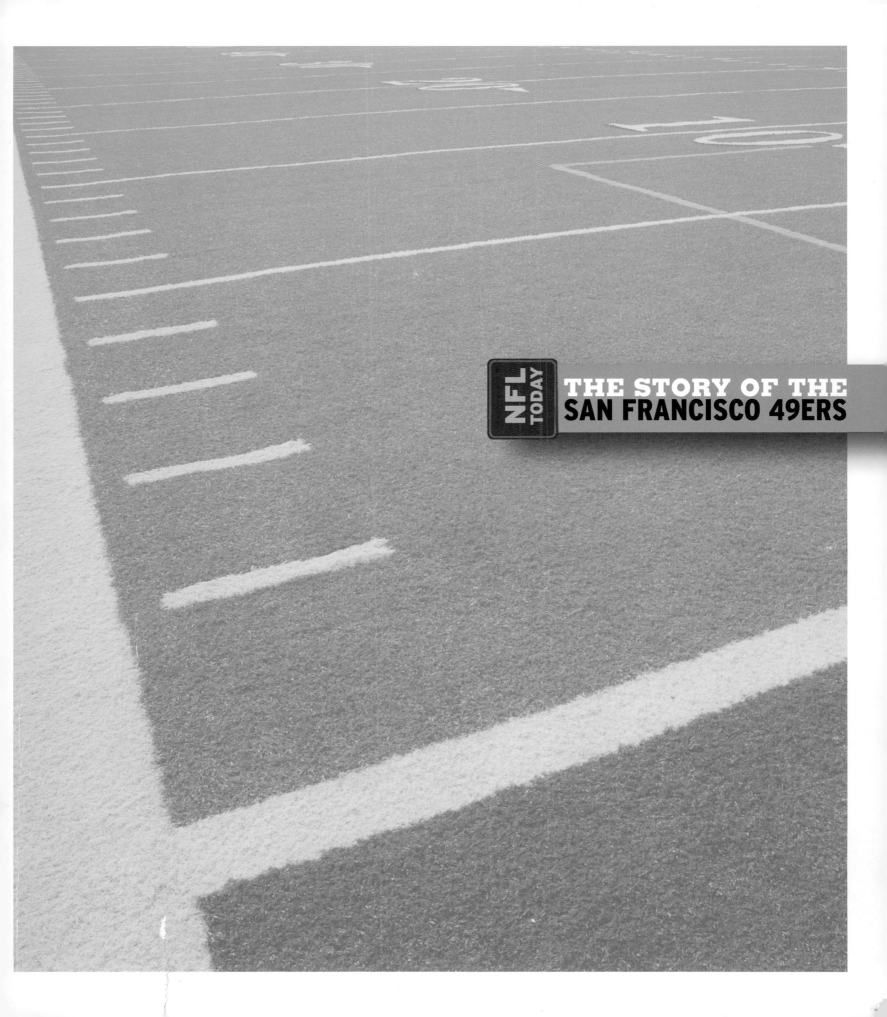

NFL TODAY

THE STORY OF THE
SAN FRANCISCO 49ERS

NFL TODAY

THE STORY OF THE SAN FRANCISCO 49ERS

LORI DITTMER

CREATIVE EDUCATION

Cover: Quarterback Joe Montana (top), running
back Frank Gore (bottom)
Page 2: Defensive tackle Bryant Young
Pages 4–5: Defensive end Fred Dean
Pages 6–7: Running back Frank Gore

. . . .

Published by Creative Education
P.O. Box 227, Mankato, Minnesota 56002
Creative Education is an imprint of
The Creative Company
www.thecreativecompany.us

Design and production by Blue Design
Design Associate: Sarah Yakawonis
Printed in the United States of America

Photographs by Corbis (Bettmann, Jeff Lewis/
Icon SMI, Michael Macor/San Francisco Chronicle),
Getty Images (James Flores/NFL, George Gojkovich,
Otto Greule Jr., Otto Greule Jr./Allsport, Andy Hayt,
Walter Iooss Jr./Sports Illustrated, Jed Jacobsohn,
Heinz Kluetmeier/Sports Illustrated, Kirby Lee/NFL,
David Madison, Ronald Martinez/Allsport, MPS/
NFL, NFL, Joseph Patronite/NFL, Frank Rippon/NFL,
George Rose, Paul Spinelli, Rick Stewart/Allsport,
Kevin Terrell, Tony Tomsic/NFL, Travel Ink, Greg Trott,
Michael Zagaris)

Library of Congress Cataloging-in-Publication Data

Dittmer, Lori.
The story of the San Francisco 49ers / by Lori
Dittmer.
p. cm. — (NFL today)
Includes index.
ISBN 978-1-58341-770-6
1. San Francisco 49ers (Football team)—History—
Juvenile literature. I. Title. II. Series.

GV956.S3D57 2009
796.332'6479461—dc22   2008022702

First Edition
9 8 7 6 5 4 3 2 1

CONTENTS

ON THE SIDELINES

MEET THE 49ERS

A BAY AREA BEGINNING

X-------------------------------------

X Among San
Francisco's defining
features are the Golden
Gate Bridge, the
famous prison island
of Alcatraz, steep city
streets—and, since
1946, a pro football
team called the 49ers.

Originally settled by Spanish explorers in 1776, San Francisco grew into a thriving California port city in the 1800s. A popular tourist destination, San Francisco has become famous for its rich history as well as its landmark, the Golden Gate Bridge. The 4,200-foot-long bridge, which opened in 1937, was named after the Golden Gate, a narrow, deep strait at the mouth of San Francisco Bay. Because the bridge is so close to the ocean, it was built to withstand the strong winds blowing in from the unpredictable Pacific.

The city's professional football team, the 49ers, is also a San Francisco landmark. Before joining the National Football League (NFL) in 1950, the 49ers, named after the miners who raced to California during the gold rush of 1849, began as part of the All-America Football Conference (AAFC) in 1946. The franchise was one of the first professional football teams based on the West Coast.

In the early 1940s, a trucking company executive named Anthony Morabito envisioned having professional football in

San Francisco. However, the NFL denied his requests to expand the league. So Morabito joined up with his brother, Victor, and together they founded the 49ers as a team in the AAFC. During the club's first four years, head coach Lawrence "Buck" Shaw assembled a talented lineup that included quarterback Frankie Albert, running back and defensive back Len Eshmont, and guard Bruno Banducci. The 49ers earned a strong combined record of 38–14–2 before the AAFC folded in 1949.

Although the AAFC was done, the 49ers were not, as the NFL absorbed three of the league's teams—the Cleveland Browns, Baltimore Colts, and the 49ers—in 1950. From 1951 to 1954, the 49ers posted a winning record every year. During those seasons, the team featured several outstanding players, including defensive tackle Leo Nomellini and Hardy Brown, a small but ferocious linebacker. Albert led the offense until quarterback Y. A. Tittle took over in 1953.

Hugh "The King" McElhenny and Joe "The Jet" Perry emerged as star running backs for the 49ers in the early 1950s. Albert had such confidence in McElhenny that he convinced Coach Shaw to put the rookie into a preseason game in 1952 despite the fact that McElhenny had just reported to training camp 24 hours earlier and didn't know the plays or even the names of his teammates. Nevertheless,

LEO NOMELLINI

DEFENSIVE TACKLE
49ERS SEASONS: 1950-63
HEIGHT: 6-FOOT-3
WEIGHT: 259 POUNDS

Leo Nomellini was the very first player the 49ers drafted after joining the NFL. But even in high school, Nomellini had no idea he would end up playing professional football. Born in Italy, Nomellini moved with his family to Chicago, Illinois, when he was a baby. As a teen, he worked to help support his family and had no time for high school sports. He began playing football after joining the Marine Corps in Cherry Point, North Carolina, and he went on to a successful college football career at the University of Minnesota. As a member of the 49ers, "The Lion" displayed rare agility, speed, and aggression throughout 174 consecutive regular-season games. One of the best pass rushers in the league, Nomellini was also versatile. The 49ers faced a crisis in 1955 when many of their players went down with injuries. To compensate for the shortage, Nomellini played tackle on both sides of the line, with little time for breathers. "He was as strong as three bulls," said Joe Perry, a 49ers running back in the 1950s. "He'd slap you on the back and knock you 20 feet."

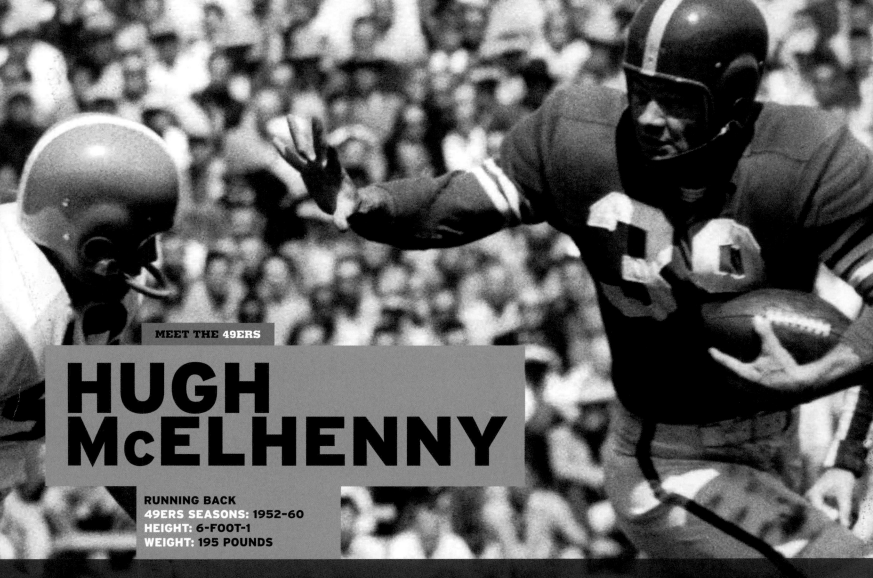

HUGH McELHENNY

RUNNING BACK
49ERS SEASONS: 1952-60
HEIGHT: 6-FOOT-1
WEIGHT: 195 POUNDS

After graduating from high school, Hugh McElhenny received a call from Los Angeles Rams assistant coach Hamp Pool. Pool wanted to know if McElhenny would like to play for the Rams, but McElhenny's father declined, sending his son to college instead. When he finished college, the young McElhenny headed to the NFL Draft, expecting to be chosen by the Rams. However, the Rams used their first pick to select quarterback Billy Wade, and the 49ers snapped up McElhenny before the Rams could choose again. McElhenny had an immediate impact on the league, using his breakaway speed to record the best rushing average (seven yards per carry) in the NFL in 1952 and earning Rookie of the Year honors. Dubbed "The King" by 49ers quarterback Frankie Albert, McElhenny ran with a distinctive style characterized by long strides and high knee action. He also had rare shiftiness in the open field, which contributed to an 89-yard run from scrimmage during his rookie season. "He could change direction on a dime," said 49ers offensive end Billy Wilson. "He had great cutting ability where other backs were just slashers."

McElhenny entered the game, took a pitch from Albert, and ran 42 yards for a touchdown. Albert also helped give Perry his nickname when the quarterback commented, "When that guy comes by to take a handoff, his slipstream darn near knocks you over. He's strictly jet-propelled." In 1953 and 1954, The Jet became the first player in professional football history to rush for more than 1,000 yards in back-to-back seasons. Fans began calling Tittle, McElhenny, Perry, and running back John Henry Johnson the "Million Dollar Backfield."

Tittle also had a competent receiver in halfback R. C. Owens, a former basketball star. The quarterback made a habit of throwing "alley-oop" passes to Owens, who would jump as high as he needed to grab the ball. "It's the strangest thing I've ever seen on a football field," one reporter noted.

In 1957, rookie quarterback John Brodie displayed his potential as the team's future starter when he filled in for the injured Tittle in a game against the mighty Baltimore Colts. With less than a minute left, Brodie threw the game-winning touchdown pass to McElhenny. Under head coach and former quarterback Frankie Albert, the 49ers went 8–4 on the season. The record was good enough for their first trip to the NFL playoffs, but they lost to the Detroit Lions, 31–27.

The 1960s were tumultuous years for the 49ers. While

The careers of San Francisco quarterbacks Y. A. Tittle (left) and John Brodie (right) were closely intertwined; after Brodie replaced Tittle as starter, Tittle mentored him as a coach. **X**

many of these seasons ended with respectable records, the 49ers could never reach the playoffs. Among the more memorable events of the decade was the advent of the "shotgun" formation. San Francisco head coach Howard "Red" Hickey introduced the formation near the end of the 1960 season. For the shotgun to work, the quarterback had to be able to scramble for yardage at times. Brodie, who was more mobile than the veteran Tittle, soon became the team's primary starter. "I held John off until the shotgun," Tittle later admitted.

In addition to running the shotgun formation, Hickey decided to rotate quarterbacks into the system, further confusing opponents. When Brodie was not in the game, Hickey used Billy Kilmer. During the 1961 season, Kilmer passed for a

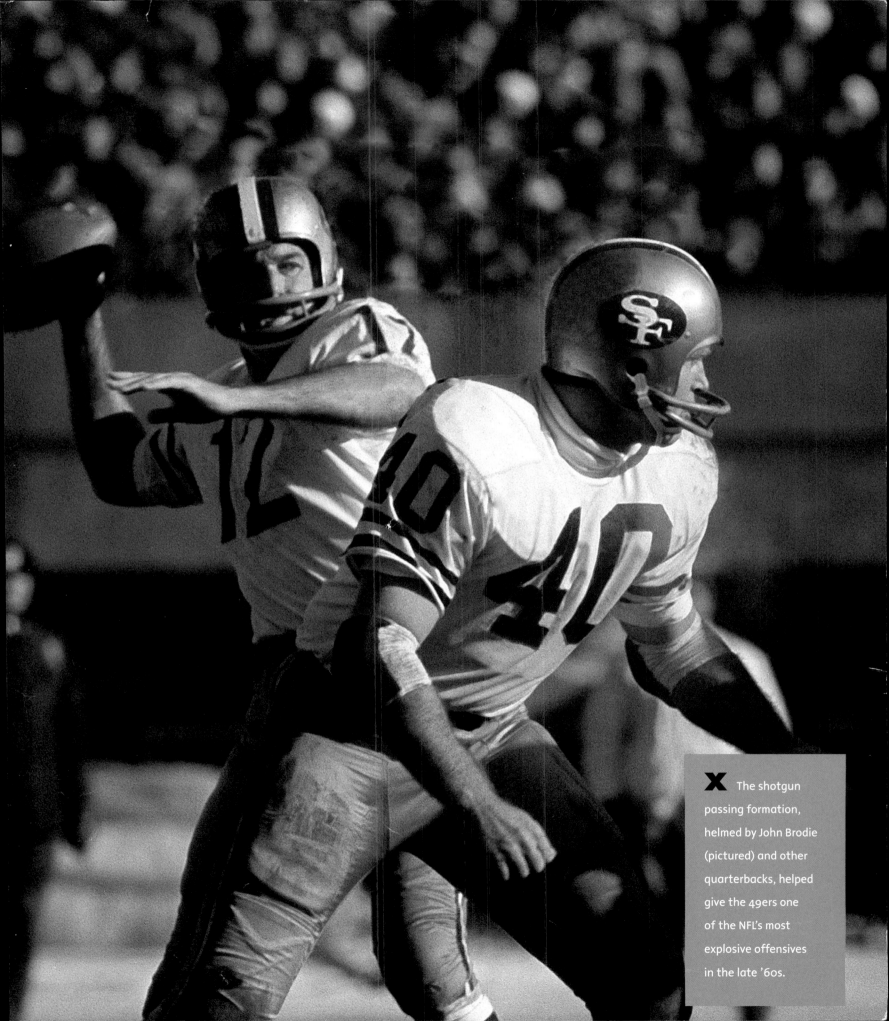

✗ The shotgun passing formation, helmed by John Brodie (pictured) and other quarterbacks, helped give the 49ers one of the NFL's most explosive offensives in the late '60s.

modest 286 yards but rushed for a whopping 509. He scored four rushing touchdowns in one game against the Minnesota Vikings, setting a team record. Hickey's third quarterback option in the shotgun was Bob "Muddy" Waters.

By the end of the 1960s, the 49ers had stocked up on new talent. Brodie and wide receiver Gene Washington led the offense, while linebacker Dave Wilcox and cornerback Jimmy Johnson anchored a solid defense. In 1968, a former NFL defensive back named Dick Nolan took over as 49ers head coach. During his first year, the team produced a 7–6–1 record. San Francisco really seemed to turn a corner in 1970, when it went 10–3–1. The 49ers reached the playoffs in 1970, 1971, and 1972, but every year, the Dallas Cowboys knocked them out.

A 4-time Pro-Bowler who scored 59 career touchdowns for San Francisco, Gene Washington became the NFL's director of football operations after retiring as a player. X

THE SHOTGUN BLASTS OFF

During a mediocre 1960 season, 49ers head coach Howard "Red" Hickey decided to spice up the team's offense by implementing a new formation. Hickey felt that defenses had decoded every offensive play, and that a new formation would catch them off-guard. The coach combined elements from several different strategies, calling his formation the "shotgun" because it sprayed receivers all over the field. "I'm an old country boy, and I used to go hunting with a shotgun," Hickey said. "How about we call it the shotgun?" In this formation, the quarterback lined up several yards behind the center, and the center tossed the ball back into his waiting hands. Running backs lined up behind but parallel to the tackles, which helped stop pass rushers and gave the quarterback more time to view the field. The 49ers introduced their new setup on November 27, 1960, in a game against the powerful Baltimore Colts and stunned their opponents with a 30–22 upset. San Francisco went on to win three of its last four games that season by using the shotgun offense.

REBUILDING WITH WALSH

x -

The 49ers' strong seasons of the early '70s were followed by several years of frustration. Powered by a solid defensive unit that included ends Cleveland Elam and Tommy Hart, the 49ers finished 8–6 in 1976. Aside from that one bright spot, however, the franchise failed to produce a winning record for the remainder of the decade.

Desperate to rebuild, the 49ers went through a carousel of coaches. Between 1976 and 1978, San Francisco tried four head coaches before bringing in Bill Walsh, who had a reputation as a great offensive mind, at the end of 1978. "When I took over the 49ers, we were acknowledged as the least-talented, least-experienced franchise in the NFL," Walsh later noted. But that was about to change.

In Walsh's first season in San Francisco, the 49ers offense revolved around quarterback Steve DeBerg. Walsh and the 49ers selected quarterback Joe Montana in the third round of the 1979 NFL Draft and took a year to groom the rookie before inserting him into the lineup. While other teams had passed on Montana because they thought he was too small and slow for the NFL, Walsh admired Montana's agility and instincts for the game. With Montana at the helm, the 49ers opened the 1980 season with three wins in a row, and they made headlines late in the season when they overcame a 35–7

X Although many players helped make the 49ers into a dynasty in the 1980s, the two men most responsible for the turnaround were quarterback Joe Montana (left) and coach Bill Walsh (right).

X A draft-day steal (not selected until the 10th round of the 1979 NFL Draft), Dwight Clark became one of Joe Montana's favorite passing targets.

halftime deficit against the New Orleans Saints. San Francisco scored 28 unanswered points to win 38–35 in the biggest comeback in NFL history.

Within three years of his hiring in San Francisco, Walsh had assembled a star-studded team that included Montana, wide receiver Dwight Clark, safety Ronnie Lott, and defensive backs Eric Wright and Dwight Hicks. The roster also included veteran linebacker Jack "Hacksaw" Reynolds, who had earned his nickname in college when he used a hacksaw and 13

X Led by players such as Jack "Hacksaw" Reynolds (number 64), the 49ers defense turned scary in the early '80s, ranking second among NFL teams in points allowed in 1981.

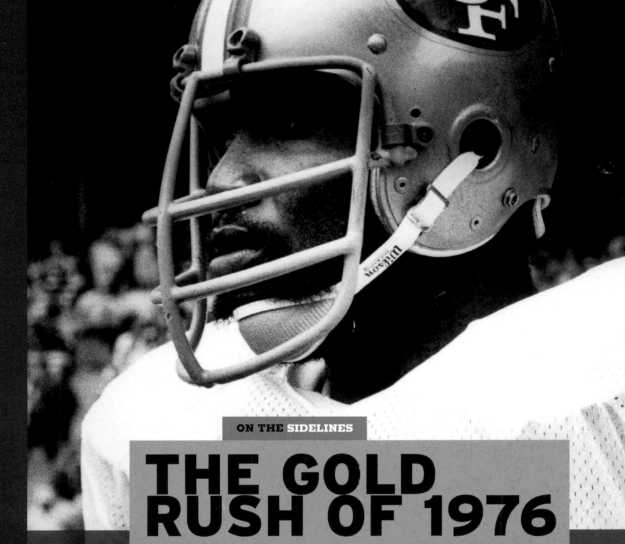

THE GOLD RUSH OF 1976

Today, the 49ers' "Gold Rush" refers to the team's cheerleading squad, but the term meant something completely different three decades ago. The 49ers struck gold in the mid-1970s when a talented group of defensive linemen came together for a record-setting season. Tommy Hart and Cedrick Hardman (pictured) manned the defensive ends, while Cleveland Elam and Jimmy Webb played the tackle spots. During the games when Hardman sat out with a broken leg, end Tony Cline filled in, and Bill Cooke also lent a hand at any position as needed. This defensive unit earned the nickname "Gold Rush." In 1976, the Gold Rush was a defensive wall, helping to limit opposing offenses to a scant 13 passing touchdowns for the year. On the season, the 49ers allowed an average of only 13.6 points per game and set a team record with 61 quarterback sacks. The team's most exhilarating game of 1976 came against the Los Angeles Rams, who were undefeated and heavily favored. Surprising everyone, the 49ers shut out the Rams 16–0, sacking quarterback James Harris 10 times in the process.

replacement blades to cut a car in half. Walsh noted that the nickname also fit the linebacker's playing style, "because he cut people down."

In the span of four years, the 49ers went from worst to first, jumping from 2–14 in 1978 to 13–3 in 1981. They claimed the National Football Conference (NFC) Western Division title for the first time since 1972, then beat the Dallas Cowboys for the NFC championship. In Super Bowl XVI against the Cincinnati Bengals, the 49ers led 20–0 by halftime. In the locker room, Walsh encouraged his players to stay focused. "I wasn't comfortable with the lead," the coach said later. "Maybe if it had been 24–0, the Bengals might have caved in, but not with the score 20–0." Although the Bengals came back with three touchdowns, the 49ers booted two field goals and held on to win 26–21. Finally, after 31 seasons, the 49ers were world champions.

The following season was a letdown in San Francisco, marred by injuries and a players' strike that shortened the schedule. The 49ers came back strong in 1983, finishing 10–6 and winning the NFC West again. The Washington Redskins knocked them off in the playoffs, but the 49ers were about to go on a tear. Before the end of the decade, San Francisco would win three more Super Bowls—beating the Miami

BILL WALSH

COACH
49ERS SEASONS: 1979-88

When Bill Walsh was hired as head coach of the 49ers in 1979, the team was in a severe slump. Walsh, who had been an assistant coach for the Oakland Raiders, Cincinnati Bengals, and San Diego Chargers, quickly rebuilt the team. After just three years, he led the 49ers to their first Super Bowl victory, and the success didn't stop there. Under Walsh's direction, the 49ers won six NFC West titles and three Super Bowls, making the 49ers the "Team of the '80s." Walsh possessed an uncanny ability to evaluate and develop players' talent, and he is credited with helping several star quarterbacks—including 49ers great Joe Montana, Ken Anderson of the Bengals, and Dan Fouts of the Chargers—fulfill their potential. Walsh was one of the first coaches to preplan series of plays in the office during the week instead of making decisions during the chaos of the game. "When we go over the game plan during the week, it doesn't look like it will work," Montana once said. "But when we get into the game and use it, it seems that the plan always works."

Dolphins 38–16 in Super Bowl XIX, the Cincinnati Bengals 20–16 in Super Bowl XXIII, and the Denver Broncos 55–10 in Super Bowl XXIV.

Montana received much of the credit for this dynasty. In 14 seasons with the 49ers, he would earn the league's Most Valuable Player (MVP) award twice. But Montana didn't win the Super Bowls alone. The star quarterback was surrounded by outstanding players, including tough running back Roger Craig and smooth receiver Jerry Rice. In 1985, Craig became the first player in league history to amass 1,000 yards rushing and 1,000 yards receiving in one season. During the last half of the 1980s, Rice emerged as a top-notch receiver; even

X Running back Roger Craig was famous for his intense running style, pumping his knees high like pistons to drive through defenders.

THE CATCH

During the 1981 season, when the 49ers went 13–3 and showed signs of greatness, they did not feel much respect from other teams. The 49ers had been a bad team in the late '70s, and a growing rivalry with the Dallas Cowboys didn't help matters. The previous year, the Cowboys had crushed San Francisco 59–14. The 49ers returned the favor in 1981, but many Cowboys players suggested that the "real" Cowboys simply hadn't shown up that day. But the 49ers continued to play well and drove all the way to the 1981 NFC Championship Game, where they faced the Cowboys once again. With only 90 seconds left in the game, the Cowboys led 27–21, and San Francisco had the ball on Dallas's 6-yard line. Quarterback Joe Montana then tossed what appeared to be a high, throwaway pass. In reality, it was a carefully planned play called "Sprint Right Option." In the back of the end zone, San Francisco wide receiver Dwight Clark soared impossibly high and snared the ball, giving the 49ers the victory. "The Catch," as the play is now known, propelled the 49ers to the first of four Super Bowl wins during the 1980s.

X In a run of dominance unequalled in NFL history, Jerry Rice led the league in receiving touchdowns in six of the eight seasons between 1986 and 1993.

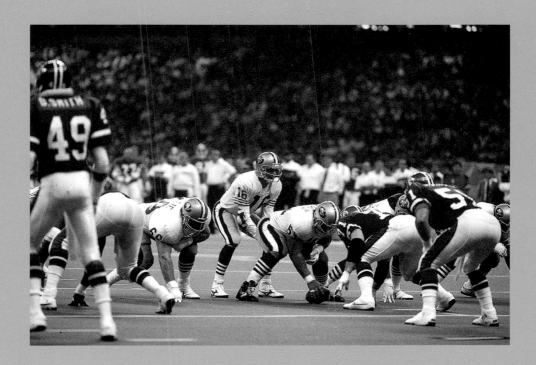

before he ended his career, many people would consider him the best receiver in NFL history. Walsh retired as head coach in 1989 after the 49ers won their third Super Bowl, having compiled a 102–63–1 record in his 10 seasons with San Francisco.

Assistant coach George Seifert replaced Walsh. Under his watch, Montana enjoyed the best season of his career in 1989, passing for 3,521 yards and 26 touchdowns. The 49ers barreled to their second consecutive Super Bowl, crushing the Broncos by 45 points. Montana had such a spectacular day, tossing five touchdown passes, three of which went to Rice, that even he started feeling a little sorry for Denver. "To have it go that well in a Super Bowl makes the game fun," said Montana, "but you get to a point when you start thinking about what it must be like to be on the other side."

X The 49ers' offensive attack was steady and unrelenting in Super Bowl XXIV after the 1989 season, scoring 13 points the first quarter and 14 points every quarter after that.

YOUNG TAKES THE TORCH

In 1990, the 49ers lost the NFC Championship Game 15–13 when the New York Giants kicked the winning field goal as time expired. The following season, Montana was sidelined by an elbow injury. Coach Seifert and the 49ers then looked to the backup quarterback who represented the team's future: Steve Young.

Young had joined the 49ers in 1987 and remained in the background for several years, learning from Montana and waiting for his chance at the starting role. "When the opportunity opened up, being a regular quarterback was no longer an option," Young said later. "I had to rise to the new standard of performance that Joe set."

At first, San Francisco fans were skeptical of their new quarterback, but Young soon won them over. His physical talents were obvious; both fast and strong-armed, he could scramble to pick up extra yards and throw with tremendous accuracy on the run. He also proved he would do whatever it took to win, including taking big hits. "Of all the players I have coached or been around, Steve was perhaps the most driven athlete I've ever seen," said 49ers quarterbacks coach Mike Holmgren.

Under Young's leadership, San Francisco's winning streak continued. In 1992, the 49ers went a league-best 14–2 before

X While he earned fame for his remarkable throwing accuracy, Steve Young also used his fleet feet to score more rushing touchdowns (43) than any other NFL quarterback in history.

JOE MONTANA

QUARTERBACK
49ERS SEASONS: 1979-92
HEIGHT: 6-FOOT-2
WEIGHT: 200 POUNDS

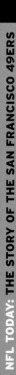

Despite leading his college team, the University of Notre Dome Fighting Irish, to a national championship during his senior year, Joe Montana was not picked by an NFL team until the third round of the 1979 Draft. Most scouts wondered if he had sufficient arm strength, and whether he was durable enough to withstand the hard knocks of professional football. But 49ers head coach Bill Walsh recognized Montana's talents. "The minute I saw Joe move, there was no question in my mind that he was the best I'd seen," said Walsh. "I knew with the offense I planned to run, Joe would be great." Walsh was right. During Montana's years with the 49ers, he led his team to 11 playoff berths and 4 Super Bowl victories. In the process, he became a master of late-game comebacks, and his "Montana Magic" helped his team come from behind in the fourth quarter to win 31 times. Always even-tempered, he earned the nickname "Joe Cool" because he kept his poise so well under pressure. By the time he retired, he was only the fifth quarterback ever to pass for more than 40,000 career yards.

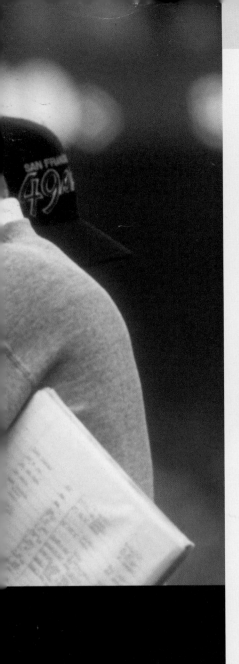

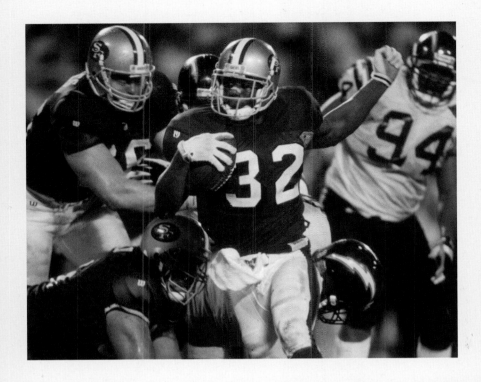

losing to the Dallas Cowboys in the NFC Championship Game.
The following year, the 49ers went 10–6 and returned to the
playoffs to face the New York Giants. In that game, 49ers
running back Ricky Watters ran for five touchdowns, setting
an NFL single-game playoff record and carrying the team to
a 44–3 win. Unfortunately, the Cowboys again ended the
49ers' Super Bowl hopes, beating them 38–21 in the NFC
Championship Game.

Everything fell into place for San Francisco in 1994. Young
embarked on one of his best seasons, throwing for 3,969
yards and 35 touchdowns. Rice set team records of his own
with 112 receptions for 1,499 yards and 13 touchdowns. The
49ers also featured a new star in lightning-fast cornerback
Deion Sanders, who was known as "Prime Time" because

X Although his
play was sometimes
overshadowed by his
hot-tempered behavior,
Ricky Watters was a
determined runner who
broke the 1,000-yard
mark in 7 NFL seasons.

of his clutch performances and love of television media attention. A two-sport athlete, Sanders had once hit a home run for the New York Yankees baseball team and scored an NFL touchdown for the Atlanta Falcons in the same week. Wearing 49ers red and gold in 1994, Sanders made six interceptions and returned three of them for touchdowns, earning the NFL's Defensive Player of the Year award. Tackle Dana Stubblefield also starred on defense, netting 8.5 quarterback sacks.

The 49ers roared into the 1994 playoffs and finally beat the Cowboys on their way to Super Bowl XXIX, where they met the San Diego Chargers. On football's biggest stage, Young tossed a Super Bowl-record six touchdown passes to lead the 49ers to a 49–26 rout and win the game's MVP award. With a Super Bowl win under his belt, Young finally felt he had escaped from under the large shadow of Joe Montana. "I've got a monkey off my back at last!" he exclaimed.

The 49ers fought their way to an 11–5 mark and the NFC West title again in 1995. The defense—including cornerback Eric Davis and linebacker Ken Norton Jr.—stood out as the team's strength, leading the league in defensive scoring and setting a team record for fewest rushing yards allowed per game (66.3). But the Green Bay Packers bounced the 49ers from the playoffs, 27–17. One year later, the same

THE WEST COAST OFFENSE

Bill Walsh often is credited with creating the "West Coast Offense," but the history of this unique offensive philosophy dates back to the San Diego Chargers teams of the 1960s, when Chargers coach Sid Gillman put five receivers into the offense. When Walsh worked as an assistant coach with the Cincinnati Bengals, he built on the idea of using more receivers on the field and giving the quarterback options for throwing either short or long passes. To succeed using this offense, receivers had to be more durable and function a bit like running backs, sometimes making a short catch and then running through traffic. "We demanded that everyone be a good receiver and that everyone have great discipline," said Walsh. "I think those are still the foundations of the offense." In Cincinnati, Walsh put the system to use when backup quarterback Virgil Carter replaced injured starter Greg Cook. Because Carter did not possess Cook's arm strength, Walsh began using the offense, hoping that a 3-yard pass could turn into a 20-yard gain. Walsh then took his offense to San Francisco, where quarterbacks Joe Montana and Steve Young gave it greater fame.

RONNIE LOTT

CORNERBACK, SAFETY
49ERS SEASONS: 1981-90
HEIGHT: 6 FEET
WEIGHT: 203 POUNDS

After being selected eighth overall in the 1981 NFL Draft, Ronnie Lott immediately earned a starting role as a rookie. Known for his speed, strength, and knowledge of the game, he quickly became a leader among the team's defensive backs, a group that became the cornerstone of San Francisco's much-improved defense. Lott played a significant role in the team's overwhelming success during the 1980s. During his rookie year, he picked off seven passes, returning three for touchdowns. He led the league in interceptions twice, with 10 in 1986 and 8 in 1991. But Lott probably became most famous for his brutal tackles. "Nobody's ever tried to hit a guy harder than he does, and he does it on a regular basis," said former New York Jets coach Pete Carroll. Lott worked hard both on and off the field to improve his play, even studying martial arts to enhance his flexibility and self-discipline. A versatile player, Lott excelled no matter where he lined up. He received 10 Pro Bowl invitations at 3 different positions: cornerback, free safety, and strong safety.

two teams met for the same playoff game. In near-freezing temperatures and pouring rain at Green Bay's Lambeau Field, the 49ers were plagued by turnovers and fumbles, losing the game 35–14.

In 1997, Steve Mariucci replaced George Seifert as San Francisco's head coach and led the 49ers to an 11-game winning streak. Running back Garrison Hearst became the first 49ers player to rush for more than 1,000 yards since 1992. Knee injuries kept Rice off the field for most of the season, but young receiver Terrell Owens picked up the slack with 936 receiving yards and 8 touchdowns. In the playoffs, though, San Francisco once again fell to the Packers, this time 23–10 in the NFC Championship Game.

The 49ers remained among the NFL's elite in 1998, racking up a 12–4 record and advancing to the playoffs for a rematch with the Green Bay Packers. With only three seconds left in the game, the 49ers finally beat the Packers when Young rifled a 25-yard touchdown strike to Owens, bringing the final score to 30–27. The next week, however, the Atlanta Falcons inched past San Francisco, 20–18.

NEW STARS,
NEW STRUGGLES

X

X In 2000 and
2001, new 49ers
quarterback Jeff Garcia
joined an elite club,
becoming only the
seventh NFL player in
history to throw at
least 30 touchdown
passes in back-to-
back seasons.

In 1999, Young suffered his fourth concussion in three
years and was lost for the year. San Francisco plummeted to
4–12, the club's first losing season in 17 years. Young then
retired, opening the door for Jeff Garcia, a small but quick
quarterback. Although he had large shoes to fill, Garcia
proved himself a worthy successor by passing for a team-
record 4,278 yards in 2000.

After accumulating 186 touchdowns and nearly
20,000 receiving yards during his 16-season career in San
Francisco, Rice left the team in 2000. Owens then became
Garcia's primary target. With his 6-foot-3 and 230-pound
frame and sure hands, Owens established himself as one of
the league's best receivers. In a game against the Chicago
Bears in December 2000, "T. O." pulled in 20 receptions,
setting a new NFL record. "He's big, he can run, and if you
play him one-on-one, he can outjump a defensive back," said
St. Louis Rams defensive coordinator Lovie Smith. "He's the
complete package."

Hearst, who had been recovering from an ankle injury for two years, returned in 2001 to rush for 1,206 yards and help the 49ers reach the playoffs. However, Green Bay once again knocked the 49ers from Super Bowl contention. In 2002, San Francisco returned to the playoffs to face the New York Giants. Although the Giants led 38–14 late in the third quarter, the 49ers charged back. During the last 17 minutes of the game, the 49ers executed the second-biggest comeback in NFL postseason history when they scored 25 points to win the game 39–38. The red-and-gold-clad San Francisco faithful cheered as though the team had just won the Super Bowl. However, the 49ers were unable to muster the same come-from-behind magic a week later, losing to the Tampa Bay Buccaneers 31–6.

The 49ers dropped to 7–9 in 2003. Then, after Owens was traded to the Philadelphia Eagles, the team fell hard from the ranks of the contenders. In 2004 and 2005, San Francisco managed a combined total of only six wins. In 2005, the 49ers welcomed new head coach Mike Nolan, son of former 49ers coach Dick Nolan. Coach Nolan looked for young players he could build around, and he soon found two. Despite splitting carries with fellow running back Kevan Barlow, rookie Frank Gore put in a solid first season in 2005, leading the team in

IF AT FIRST YOU DON'T SUCCEED...

A key component of the 49ers' Super Bowl XXIII victory over the Cincinnati Bengals, cornerback Darryl Pollard was the picture of perseverance. He went undrafted out of college in 1986 and signed with the Seattle Seahawks as a free agent, but the team cut him in training camp. The following March, the 49ers called him in and signed him, but once again, he was cut in training camp. Nearly a month later, the 49ers re-signed him to play in "replacement" games during the 24-day players' strike of 1987. When the strike was done, so was Pollard. San Francisco signed him again on August 3, 1988, and cut him again 20 days later. Just two days after that, the 49ers took him back to fill in for injured players—for five days. Finally, in September, Pollard received offers from the Seahawks and the 49ers. He stayed in San Francisco, and in the closing minutes of Super Bowl XXIII, he recovered a punt fumbled by 49ers wide receiver John Taylor at San Francisco's eight-yard-line. The recovery gave 49ers quarterback Joe Montana the chance to lead the team on the 92-yard scoring drive that won the game.

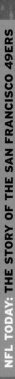
ON THE SIDELINES

SAN FRAN STADIUMS

In all their years, the 49ers have played in only two home stadiums. In 1946, the 49ers began their history in Kezar Stadium, which had previously hosted events such as motorcycle and auto races and soccer matches. For 25 years, football fans gathered at Kezar Stadium to watch their favorite team. The 49ers moved to Candlestick Park (pictured) in 1971, after the city spent $16 million renovating the stadium instead of building a new facility. The San Francisco Giants of Major League Baseball shared the stadium with the 49ers until the 2000 season, when the baseball team moved to AT&T Park. As the stadium's sponsors have changed over the years, so has its name. In 1995, Candlestick Park became 3Com Park when 3Com Corporation, a manufacturer of computer networking products, purchased naming rights to the stadium. Six years later, the park returned to its original Candlestick name for a brief period, and in 2004, Monster Cable Products Inc. paid $6 million over four years to rename the field Monster Park. When Monster's contract expired in 2008, the stadium reverted to its original name, becoming Candlestick Park once again.

rushing yards. After trying four different quarterbacks, Nolan ultimately named Alex Smith, the top overall pick of the 2005 NFL Draft, his starter for 2006.

The 49ers improved on their record in 2006, with Smith leading his team to a 7–9 finish. In Gore's first season as a starter, the 5-foot-9 and 215-pound halfback rumbled for 1,695 rushing yards, a franchise record. San Francisco ended the season on a high note, stunning the Broncos with an overtime victory that kept Denver out of the playoffs.

X In 2006, a year before he joined the 49ers, Patrick Willis won the Dick Butkus Award as America's best college linebacker at the University of Mississippi.

JERRY RICE

WIDE RECEIVER
49ERS SEASONS: 1985–2000
HEIGHT: 6-FOOT-2
WEIGHT: 200 POUNDS

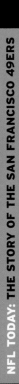

When the 49ers drafted Jerry Rice 16th overall in the 1985 NFL Draft, they hoped he would be a valuable addition to the team, but they had no way of knowing he would become one of the most prolific pass receivers in NFL history. In 1986, he led the league with 1,570 receiving yards and 15 touchdowns, but that was just the beginning. The following year, he topped the league with 23 touchdowns. Although he wasn't the fastest player in the game, Rice had deceptive speed that made him a threat to "go deep" on any play. Quarterback Joe Montana, who connected with Rice on 55 touchdowns for the 49ers, once said that Rice had a "knack for knowing when to break, when to use his speed." Rice worked hard, practicing drills as if they were real games and studying the methods of opposing defensive backs. He missed 14 games in 1997 recovering from 2 knee injuries, but he raced back to his record-setting form the following year, when he and quarterback Steve Young became the league's all-time top-scoring duo, with 80 touchdowns.

"Beating a good team at home in overtime in a tough environment just shows the growth of this team," said 49ers wide receiver Arnaz Battle.

Although the 49ers entered 2007 with high hopes, injuries derailed the team's season. Rookie linebacker Patrick Willis shone brightly through an otherwise disappointing 5–11 season by making 137 tackles and earning NFL Rookie of the Year honors. San Francisco missed the playoffs again in 2008, but still, Bay Area fans remained optimistic that such rising stars as Willis, tight end Vernon Davis, and defensive end Kentwan Balmer—the team's top pick in the 2008 NFL Draft— would soon restore San Francisco to its former glory.

The San Francisco 49ers may have started out slowly, but they have since assembled a stunning resumé of success that includes 5 Super Bowl victories and 10 NFC Championship Game appearances since 1981. And although the team has weathered some stormy seasons in recent years, today's "Niners" plan to again rise up and bring world championship number six home to the city by the bay.

INDEX